Applying to U.K. Universities

A Practical Guide for IB Students

George Graves

Acknowledgements

I would like to thank my daughter Leonie Elliott-Graves for patiently reading through the text and presenting it in a user-friendly format.

Many thanks also to Lydia for proof reading and correcting punctuation and for providing encouragement and support.

I must also thank the many academic staff and admissions officers who gave up their time to provide the invaluable information for this book.

Author

George Graves has taught Economics in Greece since 1973 and has been involved in University applications for over 30 years.

Dedication

I dedicate this book to Konstantinos Malamas and all the other applicants who I have helped. I wish them every success with their studies.

Table of Contents

Introduction

How times change..... I remember in 1970 receiving an offer by post from the LSE to study BSc. Economics. Although I was taking three A-Levels, the offer was for two B grades in any two subjects, none of which were Mathematics. At the time, I was not aware of the existence of the IB and did not meet anyone at University who had a background in it so I do not know what the equivalent IB offer would have been. Nowadays, you need a predicted grade of A* in A level maths or a 7 in Higher Level Maths to be even considered for an offer. The typical offer now is 38 points in the IB Diploma with 7, 6, 6 at Higher Level with the 7 in Maths. In fact this is the easy part; the difficult part is in obtaining the offer. The LSE, like many Russell Group universities, has an abundance of applications from highly qualified students and could fill the number of places on their courses many times over with students who either have or are likely to gain well above the typical offer.

I am often approached by IB students who say that, even though, they had a prediction of 38 and 7, 6, 6 they failed to get an offer from the LSE or some other competitive university. When I reply that I know of two applicants who had predictions of 43 and 7, 7, 7 at Higher Level yet did not receive offers from two or three of their choices, they feel slightly better, but inevitably ask 'why'? 'What do you need to get an offer?'

Students often think that, if they have the predicted grades required for a course, they will automatically receive an offer for that course. Unfortunately, the reality is not quite so simple. There are a variety of factors that universities take into consideration and these may differ between universities and even within them. Different departments will have different criteria and these will vary between universities. Clearly, there is no one formula that can be applied in order to ensure a successful application. Despite this, there are some key features of a candidate's application form that will be considered and these need to be presented in the best possible way.

This guide introduces the IB applicant to the application process for UK universities through UCAS and offers clear guidance on how to complete the application form. Certain sections of the application form will be dealt with separately because they are potentially of greater significance.

Chapter 1 provides you with a step-by-step guide on how to complete your UCAS application for courses in U.K. universities. In this chapter, you will find a check list of what you need to do as well as advice on how to make your application stand out.

Chapter 2 deals with your university course choices in depth. It describes the process of choosing the courses and universities you will apply to and gives advice on the smartest way to choose your options.

Chapter 3 evaluates the relative importance of the Personal Statement in university applications and provides a guide on how to write a powerful and appropriate Personal

Statement. In this chapter, you will also find some examples of Personal Statements of successful applicants.

Chapter 4 deals specifically with applying to Oxford, Cambridge and Medicine courses. These courses have special requirements and the chapter provides a step-by-step guide and advice on applying to these courses. The chapter also details the interview process for these courses and provides advice for potential applicants.

Chapter 5 provides first hand advice and opinions from a selection of university tutors and Admissions Officers from some of the most popular U.K. universities. They specify what they look for in an application. Even though their opinions vary somewhat, useful conclusions can be made from their statements.

Chapter 6 presents a case study, which records the process of selecting, applying to and securing a place on a university course. This will give you a clear sense of what to expect and when to begin your own process of applying to universities.

I have written this book with evidence and experience collected from years of advising and helping I.B. students applying to universities. I hope you find it useful and wish you luck with your application.

Chapter 1: UCAS Application Process

In order to apply to officially recognised institutions in the UK to study for undergraduate courses, it is necessary to submit an application online through the central agency: Universities and Colleges Admissions Service (UCAS). Most schools provide assistance to their applicants so that the majority apply through the school supported option. This involves a school faculty member undertaking the task of providing a reference for the applicant. It is possible, however, for the applicant to apply as an individual and to request a reference from someone who is not necessarily connected with the applicant's school. This might be the case when the applicant has left school and decides to apply at a later date. Either way, the application process is as follows:

Step 1: Registration on the UCAS site

This involves completing some personal data (name, address etc), entering your email address and a password. A verification code will then be sent to your email address and with this you will be able to log onto to your application form using the ID provided and your password.

Step 2: Log on

When you log on as a school supported applicant you need to have a Buzzword that will be provided by your school.

The various sections of the application form will now be accessible to you so that you can begin filling these in.

The first section is your personal details, some of which will already have been recorded. You should proceed to complete this section and then tick the box 'section completed'. Your information will be saved and you can always return and edit the information; for example, if your address or telephone number changes.

The remaining sections are:

- Choices
- Education
- Employment
- Personal Statement
- Reference

Step 3

Apart from the reference, which will be completed either by your school counsellor or someone whom you have nominated, you can now proceed to complete these sections in any order.

Choices will be dealt with in Chapter 2.

Starting with **education**, you will be requested to enter the schools that you have attended over recent years and particularly those where you have sat for official exams and where you will be taking your IB Diploma. The potentially tricky part here is to register your qualifications in chronological order and make sure that the dates match up with a school you attended at that date. It is quite simple to register mainstream qualifications such as IGCSE, IELTS, Cambridge Proficiency etc. as these can be found in the drop down box provided. European applicants, however, may have difficulty finding language qualifications such as Delf, Dalf A1 etc. for French and, similarly, for other languages. These should be listed by ticking 'other' on the drop down box and entering the qualification. The process is similar for national equivalents to GCSE exams. Some of these may be listed such as the Apolytirion of Gymnasium taken by Greek pupils at age 16. If not officially listed, such qualifications should be included using the 'other' box.

Make sure that you look carefully at the list of qualifications that can be recorded because you might fail to record a music or dance or language certificate that you have gained.

> **I cannot emphasise enough** that one of the most important selection criteria is evidence of academic ability so you need to include as much evidence of this as possible. Actual grades are far more convincing than predicted grades.

When you have entered all the qualifications that you have taken, you then need to register the IB Diploma subjects or certificates that you are going to be taking. These are also available from the relevant drop down boxes. Remember to include the Extended Essay and TOK with your six Diploma subjects. In the results box you will enter 'pending'.

Any other qualifications, such as language exams, IELTS, SAT, AP etc., that you plan to take should also be recorded. Make sure that the date that you will be taking these exams corresponds to a date that you will be in attendance at a school or educational establishment listed in this section. Otherwise, UCAS gets confused and will not allow you to enter the subject.

The next section is **employment**. Do not be intimidated by this and think that you have to have an entry here. This section is specifically for applicants who have worked after leaving school and who have decided to apply to university. It also applies to applicants who have taken a gap year in order to gain work experience. For the typical IB applicant, who is still at school, there is no expectation of having employment experience. Some applicants might choose to enter holiday employment details here or part time employment, but this can also be mentioned in the personal statement. Leaving this section blank will in no way jeopardise your application. However, if you do happen to have relevant work experience you should list it here with your employers name and address in case a university wishes to contact them.

The importance of any employment is with respect to the experience it provides and how it affects your suitability to the course, so if it is to be at all useful to your application, it needs to be discussed in your personal statement.

The next section is **Personal Statement** and will be dealt with in a Chapter 3.

The final section is the **Reference, which** needs to be completed by someone who is familiar with your academic potential and performance as well as your suitability for undergraduate studies. The majority of IB applications are through their respective IB schools and so the referee is likely to be a teacher or counsellor who has some experience and knowledge in this area. The person(s) responsible usually collects information from your teachers and collates this to form an overall opinion regarding your academic performance to date, your predicted grades, your contribution to the school community and suitability for the chosen courses of study. As a student you have no direct influence on what will be written by your referee, but you can improve your profile by performing well in mock exams and by showing a willingness to participate in school and CAS activities. Some diplomatic skills might be necessary on your part in order to secure the most positive and encouraging references, but be warned that most teachers get fed up with students constantly pestering them about their predicted grades. If you want a favourable prediction, make sure that you do your homework on time, meet all the IB deadlines and revise properly for tests and exams.

Ideally, the reference should complement your personal statement. Therefore, it is advisable for applicants to competitive courses, who have the necessary academic credentials, to work closely with their referee in order to decide what to include in the personal statement and what to mention in the reference.

Remember that schools gain prestige if their students receive offers from competitive universities but lose prestige if they fail to achieve the offer. You and your school need to be realistic about your potential. If you are deemed to be a valid applicant for a highly competitive course, you need to work closely with your referee to present your application in the most favourable light. You must ensure that your school supports your course choices and that the predicted grades and comments are appropriate to the entry requirements for the courses. If a course requires a 7 in Higher Level Maths and your teacher is only prepared to predict a 5 or even a 6, then to include it is a wasted choice.

If you genuinely feel that your school underestimates your qualities and abilities, you can try to make a claim in the personal statement. Advice on this will be given in the relevant chapter.

When your application is completed, it will be sent to UCAS after you or your school has paid the application fee.

UCAS will then send a copy of your form to each of your chosen courses. When the university receives your form, it has no information about your other choices but simply knows that you have applied to that university for a particular course.

On receipt of your application, most universities will acknowledge this by communicating to you with the method that you have registered as your preference e.g. by email.

UCAS will also send an acknowledgement letter by post which will include a possibly revised application number. This number, together with your password, allows you to log on to **'track'** so that you can, literally, track the progress of your application. To do so requires that you click on 'choices' and information regarding the status of your application will be shown.

In the event that an offer of a place has been made, this will be indicated and the conditions of the offer together with a letter can be accessed. If the university course is unwilling to give you an offer, this will be indicated as an 'unsuccessful' notification, popularly known as a rejection. When all decisions have been made from all of your choices, you will be given a date by which you have to reply. You are requested to accept one of your offers as a 'firm choice', one as 'insurance' and to decline the rest. Logically, you will accept the most preferred offer as your 'firm' and a lower offer as your 'insurance'.

It is usual for the university course to notify applicants of a decision and for UCAS to do likewise, advising that the status of the application has changed.

> However, you are advised to **track your application regularly** for updates. Friday evening seems to be the most frequent time for such updates.

Having made your decision, you then need to wait for your results in order to see if you have met the conditions of the offer. IB applicants have a considerable advantage over A-Level applicants because the IB results are published on 5th July whereas A-Level results are usually published around the 15th of August. This means that successful applicants can confirm their places early and proceed to make arrangements regarding accommodation etc.

> **If an applicant has narrowly missed the conditions of the offer,** the university may nevertheless be willing to confirm a place depending on the number of successful IB applicants and past experience.

Usually, failure to meet an offer requires that the applicant has to wait for A-Level results before the university is able to make a decision. When IB results are published, it is well worth contacting the university course, even if the conditions have not been met, to see what the prospects are for acceptance. It is also possible to discuss whether a re-mark for a subject or subjects should be considered. If possible, the assistance of the school and the referee should be enlisted for these negotiations.

Be advised that **re-marks** can lead to either an improved grade or a lower grade or no change, so they **should only be considered if the existing mark is close to the upper grade boundary!**

E.g.: if the candidate needs a 6 and the grade 5 boundary is 52 to 64, then a re-mark should only be considered if the actual grade is above 58 so as to minimise the risk of a reduced grade.

Important dates

September: The application process starts.

15th October: The deadline for applications to Oxford or Cambridge and for Medicine, Dentistry and Veterinary Science.

- ❖ In order to meet the deadline, it is necessary to complete your sections of the form well before this date in order to give your referee enough time to write your reference.

15th January: The closing date for most other courses.

- ❖ It is always advisable to apply well before this deadline. If you are applying to competitive courses, but not to Oxbridge or Medicine, it is advisable to send your application towards the end of **October** or early **November**. If your application is strong, there is a good chance that you might receive an offer before the Christmas break.
- ❖ Some universities look at applications as they come in and like to send out replies as they go along, while others wait until all the applications are in before making decisions. Either way, all of your choices are obliged to reply to you by the end of March or some other specified date (e.g. if you use 'extra' or apply after the January deadline).

Offers will be '**conditional**' unless you already have all of the qualifications that you are going to present, in which case, you will either receive an '**unconditional**' offer or a rejection. A conditional offer will specify the conditions with respect to the IB Diploma score that is required together with any other pending qualifications. The conditions will vary from university to university and course-to-course depending on how competitive the course is and how the IB is perceived.

A typical offer will include an overall IB Diploma score together with specific subject scores.

- e.g. **38** points overall with **7, 6, 6,** at Higher Level and **no** subject below **5**.

Competitive Economics courses will usually specify 7 in HL Maths.

Most universities are happy for the overall score to include the bonus points for the Extended Essay and TOK, but some might exclude these or include only 1 of the 3 bonus points.

- E.g. City University gives a typical offer for Business Studies or Management of 35 but only includes 1 bonus point in this total.

Even though the closing date for applications is 15th January, many universities will accept applications after this date.

However, the most competitive **Russell Group courses will not usually accept late applications!**

If, for any reason, you decide to add a choice or submit an application after the deadline, you should check that the university is willing to consider late applications. A good indicator of this is whether the course is available on '**Extra**'. An 'extra' listing means that the course is open for applications and is available for applicants who have been unsuccessful with all their applications. This year 'extra' begins on **25th February.**

Unsuccessful applicants are allowed to make an 'extra' choice and if they are unable to secure an offer through 'extra', there is always the possibility of finding a place through '**clearing**'.

The 'clearing' process begins a few days after the publication of the A-Level results in the middle of August. If you have not had confirmation of a place by this time, you will be eligible to enter 'clearing'. The aim is to find a course that interests you and which is willing to offer you a place with the grades that you have. The internet provides various sites which list available courses, but these will not necessarily keep up with the changing situation. The best advice is to make a list of telephone numbers for the courses that interest you and contact them by phone to see if they are willing to accept you.

> **Make sure that the person you are speaking to realises that you are an IB applicant** and that they are familiar with the IB grading system as the majority of clearing calls are from A-Level applicants.

If your grades are acceptable, you will be able to apply for the course on UCAS using your clearing number to secure your place. The university will then notify you that you have been accepted and informed of the dates for registration etc. In order to register for the course, you will have to make an arrangement for payment of fees and you will be required to provide proof of your qualifications that meet the conditions of the offer. The main document will be the IB Diploma, but you should also have any other certificates that might be relevant, such as the IELTS.

Most universities invite new students to an introductory or '**Fresher's**' week where you get to know your classmates and find your way around. Once you reach this stage, you will have no further need for my guide and I wish you good luck with your studies.

Chapter 2: Choices

The choices you have

You can select up to **five** courses on your application.

I stress courses, rather than universities, because it is possible that you might want to apply to two or more courses at the same university. This will be the case if you have a particular university that you want to attend and which has more than one course that interests you.

- e.g.: where a university offers an Economics course and a Management course, which are both appealing to you.

> **Make sure,** however, **that the departments are separate** and are assessed by a different admissions team.

Making your choices

Before you finalise your choices you need to engage in extensive research. You need to have some idea of the location of the universities that you are selecting. Remember that you will be spending a minimum of 3 years there!

- ✓ Make sure that you are aware of the campus facilities that are provided and try to get some idea of student satisfaction by visiting social media sites where current students discuss their views regarding the university and the area.
- ✓ Decide whether you prefer a city location or a campus. See what type of accommodation is offered, how close it is to the university, get some idea of what private accommodation is available and the typical cost. You must ask yourself the question 'Do I want to be in London for 3 years?' or 'Do I want to be in the countryside for 3 years?'

Getting to know the university

I would encourage you to try and visit the universities that interest you as most universities have several open days available for such visits. If you cannot make the official open days, most universities will agree to allow you to visit at some other time and might even be able to arrange for you to speak with someone about your chosen course.

> **It is always best to visit universities during term time** when there are students about so that you can get a better feel of the atmosphere.
>
> Personally, I look out for happy faces, interaction within groups and whether people are wandering around aimlessly or moving purposefully toward their destination.

If you have a friend or family member at the university, so much the better, as they will be able to give you a more intimate tour of the campus.

Choosing a particular course

As well as a university, you have to choose a course and this is often a very daunting prospect. Some lucky applicants know exactly what they want to study and have selected the relevant Higher Level subjects with this in mind. Their parents are in full agreement and they have researched the most suitable universities appropriate for their academic potential and expectations.

Unfortunately, many applicants are still undecided or are torn between two or more interests which are not very compatible. The problem in such cases is how to write a personal statement that is applicable to more than one type of course.

If the courses are related, such as: Business/Management/Economics or Mechanical Engineering/Robotics/Manufacturing or International Relations/Politics/History, it is quite possible to write a suitable personal statement. However, if the courses are less well related like Law/History or Psychology/Politics or Chemistry/Geography, it will take a wizard to be able to write a suitable personal statement. In such cases of diverse interest, it is advisable to try to find combined courses that might accommodate both subjects. Alternatively, decide which your preferred subject is and gear the personal statement to that subject, but mention your interest in the other subject. More and more universities are offering dual interest courses where you can decide which course to specialise in after the first year.

- e.g.: UCL has recently introduced an Arts and Science course which allows you to decide which path to follow in your second year. You need a higher level Arts/Humanities subject and a higher level Science subject to be considered for this course.

Some applicants feel obliged to study what their parents want them to, rather than their own preference, and end up being unhappy at university and possibly even failing.

> **It is very important that you are sure of what you want to study** and you must insist on this. Changing courses once you have started is difficult and should be avoided.

If you are unsure of what you want to study, you should try to find general courses that allow scope for specialisation after the first year.

For those applicants who know exactly what they want to study the course choices will be easier but will still require careful consideration and extensive research. The first step should be to log on to UCAS and conduct a course search. This will give you some idea of what is available, and where, as well as the variety of combined or joint courses. For combined courses like History and Politics, the 'and' implies a fairly equal division between the two subjects. In contrast, if the course is History with Politics, the 'with' implies a greater History content than Politics. Courses with the exact same name will be different at each university; therefore, you need to look at the course content and the optional subjects available so as to achieve the mix that suits you best. This information will be listed in the prospectus or accessible from the university internet site. You might be interested in the ratio of exam results to coursework for your final grade. IB applicants are experienced with coursework and therefore might prefer a course with a greater proportion of coursework. Similarly, IB applicants who did well in their Extended Essay might prefer a course that has a dissertation option. A dissertation will usually be 10,000 words and can be selected in place of an examined subject.

> Before finalising your choices you need to **look carefully at the entry requirements.**

Virtually all universities are well versed in the IB and this is reflected in the prospectus or web site, which list the typical IB requirement for the course. You need to make sure that you meet any subject requirements. There is no point in applying to UCL to study Mechanical Engineering if you are not offering Maths and Physics at Higher Level; similarly, most competitive Economics courses require Higher Level Maths and applicants for Medicine normally need Higher Level Chemistry and Biology. These requirements may differ between universities and you need to check carefully. If your subjects are appropriate, you still need to make a realistic assessment of your likely grades and the likely grade prediction that you will have. Bear in mind that, for the most competitive courses, the entry requirement stated constitutes a minimum and that most successful applicants will have predicted grades much higher than this minimum. An optimistic prediction of 37 does not mean that you will receive an offer for a course that asks for 37. Courses that ask for 37 and above will be looking for academic potential at a higher level as well as an interesting profile. Many of these courses can fill their places three times over with applicants who have two or more points above their typical offer.

> When making your choices you need to realistically **assess your chances of an offer** and you need to **include at least one safety or insurance choice**.

As well as the overall requirements, you must consider any subject specific requirements for the course. If, for example, a course requires 7 in Higher Level Maths and you have no chance of gaining a 7, you should not apply for the course. You also need to check if there are any other requirements for the course. Some Law courses require you to take the LNAT exam and some Medicine courses require UKCAT. Similarly, for social sciences and humanities most Oxbridge colleges will require a good score on the TSA. These are subject area specific aptitude tests and you are advised to visit the test web sites in order to do some practice questions to see how well you can perform. If it is clear that you do not have an aptitude for these tests, you need to select courses that do not require them.

Some Strategic Advice

If you send your application before the 15th of October and you are not applying for medical related courses, it will be assumed that you have applied to Oxford or Cambridge even though your other choices are not visible to each university course that you have applied to. Some applicants, who have not included Oxbridge, think that sending an early application before the 15th of October will impress the universities who are tricked into thinking that you have applied to Oxbridge. The vast majority of admissions officers that I have spoken to are not tricked or impressed by this strategy and there is also the possibility that the strategy could even backfire. Although no admissions tutor has admitted it, there is circumstantial evidence to suggest that some highly competitive courses might reject applicants who appear to have included Oxford or Cambridge. I know of several cases where quite strong Oxbridge applicants received rejections in November from one or two of their other choices.

Despite the absence of any firm evidence beyond the anecdotal, my advice is not to send your application before the 15th of October, unless you *are* applying to Oxbridge; this is particularly important if you are applying to very competitive courses. However, you should aim to send your application as soon after the 15th as possible. Many universities look at applications as they come in. Therefore, by sending your application early, you increase the chances of your application being considered quickly which improves your chances of getting an early offer i.e. before the Christmas break. If you send your application at the last minute, just before the 15th of January deadline, you should not expect to have a quick reply from your choices. In addition, there will possibly be fewer offers available as some universities will have already given out some offers.

However, there might be a good reason for delaying your application; for example, if you are undecided about your choices or if you are waiting for some internal school results in order to improve your predicted grades. If there is no such reason you are advised to send your application as early as possible.

Remember that you do not have to make all your choices together. You can send your application with less than five choices recorded and you have the opportunity of adding choices at a later date.

This might be a sensible strategy if you are unsure about some of your choices or if you want to 'test the water' to see what response you get from your initial choices.

Some schools might insist that you make all five choices at once, but you are not obliged to do this. You might only be interested in three or four courses or you might want to leave a choice open for later use.

Strategic Tip: Look at this year's clearing information

In mid-August of the year that your application will be prepared, you have a golden opportunity of seeing which courses are oversubscribed and which might be less in demand or more flexible when results are published. Even though you will not be participating in that year's clearing, the clearing information available will give you a good insight into what you can expect for next year. If your first choice course does not come out in clearing, then you can assume that it is highly competitive and will fill all its places with those holding the offer as a firm or insurance choice. This might mean, however, that the course selectors could possibly apply some flexibility at the results stage, being more willing to fill places with students holding an offer than to court new students through clearing. For some universities it is a matter of pride that they do not offer courses in clearing.

If a course that interests you does come out in clearing and accepts a slightly lower entry grade, this suggests that there will be some flexibility at the results stage. Therefore, if you are predicted to meet the standard requirement you are likely to secure an offer. The longer a course remains in clearing, the greater the chances of getting an offer when you apply. By the same token, a course that remains in clearing for a relatively long time suggests that it is undersubscribed and that you need not use one of your choices to apply to it. What applies this year is likely to be similar next year so you can confidently expect that such courses will be available in clearing next year.

How does this help?

Assume that you have the following replies from your choices:

Choice A: 36 points

Choice B: 35 points

Choice C: 26 points

Choice D & E: unsuccessful.

Assuming that **A, B** and **C** is the order of your preferences, you face the dilemma of what to accept as your insurance. Conventional wisdom would suggest that you accept **A** as your firm and **C** as your insurance. If **B** is accepted as your insurance, you run the risk of not being accepted at either choice if you get 34 points or less. This is indeed the case, but if you end up with 35 points and are not accepted at your firm choice, you will be obliged to accept **C** and will miss out on **B**, which you prefer to **C**.

If your summer clearing research has indicated that course **C** remained in clearing for more than two weeks and accepted applicants with 25 points, it ceases to be too risky to accept **A** firmly and **B** as your insurance, because the chances are that you will be able to get into **C** through clearing. Even if **C** is not available, a similar course is most likely to be available through clearing.

Each year's 'clearing' is a very good indicator of the relative difficulty of getting an offer or being accepted in the following academic year and I strongly advise you to use the information when you are making your choices.

Value for Money

With many universities charging the maximum fee, it is quite difficult to judge where you will get the best value for money and equally difficult to estimate this.

> **What to consider:** Quality of teaching, hours of instruction per week, tutorial and small group provision and availability of bursaries and scholarships are all-important factors here.

In order to attract high calibre applicants, some universities offer financial assistance (through special offers of reduced fees or bursaries) to students who have high predicted grades hoping to induce applicants to commit to them as their firm choice. One Russell Group university actually converted conditional offers to unconditional if high scoring applicants made it their firm choice.

These inducements are likely to increase as universities want to attract high scoring applicants and you should research them carefully to take advantage of what is being offered. Several universities are making an effort to move up the rankings and this is assisted by increasing their average grade intake. Also, high scoring applicants help a university to improve its profile. The subsequent performance of these students, who are likely to secure good degrees, will further enhance the university's ranking.

Chapter 3: The Personal Statement

This is probably the trickiest part of the application process and can easily turn into a 'catch-22' situation. This is an area where everybody seems to have an opinion; the applicant is often bombarded with advice, often contradictory. The universities themselves sometimes contribute to the confusion by giving misleading advice.

- e.g. One university prospectus included advice that it is important, in the personal statement, to indicate a clear interest and commitment to that university. This is misleading advice since the same personal statement is read by all the applicants' choices.

The majority of admissions officers and tutors claim that the personal statement is of utmost importance and this is clearly true for courses that are oversubscribed and which receive hundreds more high quality applications than available places. In such cases, the personal statement is the only way to distinguish between, otherwise, equally good candidates. It might be useful here to make a distinction between the Russell Group [1] universities and the rest. The Russell Group are the most competitive and, some would say, elitist of UK universities and their admissions policies are typically different from other universities. They are frequently accused of favouring independent schools over state schools. In fact, many surveys have been conducted to establish whether this is the case.

> The majority of IB applicants are in a separate category.
>
> Even if there is **a private school bias, this will not**
>
> **disadvantage the average IB applicant.**

My interest here is not to investigate the possible bias against state schools, but to try to establish the use that is made of the personal statement by universities and the extent to which their selection procedures are objective and consistent.

> It is clear that **the personal statement plays a much more important role in the admissions process for the Russell Group universities**, but even here its role is ambiguous.

---

[1] "The Russell Group represents 24 leading UK universities which are committed to maintaining the very best research, an outstanding teaching and learning experience and unrivalled links with business and the public sector." *Russell Group Website*, russellgroup.ac.uk, 1 May 2014.

However, this is not true for the vast majority of courses, many of which are undersubscribed. These are typically the courses that appear as 'extra'. They accept applicants after the January 15th closing date and usually list, in 'clearing', available courses with places to fill.

For these courses, the personal statement does not count for much and is only really used to decide borderline cases. If an applicant has the actual or predicted grades, an offer will usually be given and it is quite possible that the personal statement will not be read at all. One admissions officer confided in me that she only read the personal statement for applicants who did not present a wholly convincing academic profile. Her opinion was that there is very little 'original truth' in these statements and that most are predictable. What the university wants to see is evidence of academic ability, which will enable the applicant to complete the course successfully.

A strong personal statement and a predicted IB score of 38 may secure an *offer* for a place on a competitive course, but it is the actual score of 38 that will secure the *place*. It is academic achievement that the universities are most interested in. This is clearly reflected by the 'adjustment' process that has recently been introduced, allowing candidates who do better than expected request consideration for courses that have a higher entry requirement than their firm choice.

The aim of this chapter is to provide a realistic appraisal of the role of the personal statement and to offer practical guidelines on how to go about producing a convincing and appropriate statement (including what to avoid and how to be original). Hopefully, I will be able to dispel much of the ***mythology*** surrounding this topic and I will provide specific advice for IB applicants that will give them an advantage over other applicants. My opinions will be supported by evidence from actual admissions officers and tutors and the findings of two important studies: the Pearson Think Tank, published in 2013, and the Sutton Trust.

Myths

The first myth that I would like to address is the necessity for the statement to be completely personal, in the sense that it is exclusively the product of the applicant.

> **No professional universities counsellor would allow applicants to send off their original personal statements without at least some suggestions and corrections.**

Many private schools have teams of advisors who provide support and guidance for the writing of the personal statement. Consequently, the end result, frequently, bears little resemblance to the applicant's first draft. Left to themselves, applicants would tend to produce poorly written descriptive accounts of their achievements, relying on clichés and exaggerated attributes.

The rewriting of the personal statement is, therefore, necessary for the majority of those applying to the most competitive courses. Unfortunately, this raises the bar for all applicants. As long as nothing has been copied directly from some written source, it is impossible for UCAS or a university to know if a personal statement is the applicant's own work. This puts the applicant who wants to 'do it alone' at a serious disadvantage and makes the writing of a truly original and interesting personal statement so much more difficult.

A university might suspect that a statement is too sophisticated to be the work of the applicant, but failing to detect evidence of plagiarism, it will have to give the applicant the benefit of the doubt. In any case, experienced counsellors and advisers are good at writing convincing statements for prospective applicants and competitive universities are used to reading statements that have been 'processed'. In fact, some admissions tutors would be offended if an applicant did not take the personal statement seriously enough to seek outside advice and help. The danger is that the personal statement ceases to be a useful criterion for admissions and will be increasingly ignored by some universities.

The **Pearson Think Tank** has some very pertinent quotes, provided anonymously, by actual Russell Group University admissions officers. Some of these views and the opinions of the study are as follows:[2]

> "The use and importance of personal statements was highly variable both between and within institutions. In some universities, and for some less competitive courses, they were not used at all in assessment of the application, whilst in others these were important in differentiating between applicants and gaining a sense of their suitability for the course."

> 'Sometimes it makes no difference; sometimes it makes all the difference.'

(Admissions staff member, University A).

---

[2] Candy, S., *(Un)informed Choices? University admissions* practices and social mobility. London: Pearson, 2013.

'I don't see it would make any difference if they weren't there frankly, because those who are told what to write and all the rest of it … and not all of them are true.'

(Admissions staff member, University D)

'I don't like personal statements, there is too much evidence, anecdotal evidence about the role of teachers in personal statements and there has to be a concern that the better, the more privileged the school, the more help is on hand to creating personal statements, that's why we down-weight them. We distrust them.'

(Academic tutor, University B)

'We do assume that the applicant has written it themselves and that it is something valid to look at.'

(Admissions staff member, University C)

"I've spoken to Heads of private schools about the question of how much help they give students in writing statements, they said, 'well they're paying £7,000 a term of course we give them a lot of help, that's what they're paying for',".

(Admissions staff member, University D)

> 'We have so many overqualified applicants if we just went on grades we'd accept everybody, so we must use the personal statement … it tells me something about the applicant, it tells me something about the way they view the subject and the kind of work they want to do, and that is important for a subject like politics which can be taught in a number of different ways.'

(Academic tutor, University A)

The above selection of quotes gives some indication of the diversity of opinion regarding the personal statement. It would appear that academic admissions tutors attach more importance to it than do general admissions staff.

The research by **Dr. Steven Jones of Manchester University** for the **Sutton Trust** confirms the ambiguity of the personal statement, and although its perspective is more interested in the disadvantage to state schools, it also provides evidence of inconsistency in its use as an admissions criterion. It recommends that "Personal statements should be more than an excuse to highlight past advantages. Applicants should outline how they might contribute to campus life, and universities should make it clear that applicants are not penalised for lacking opportunities in the past due to family circumstances."[3]

The **Pearson Think Tank** recommendation is that: "The use of personal statements, and references from schools, within admissions assessment should be ended. In order to increase the transparency of decision-making processes and improve the equity of the selection process at both an institutional and a sector level, all universities should implement a centralised admissions process. This would remove differential subjective assessments and value judgements made by academic staff across faculties and departments." [4]

Universities claim that they are looking for a truthful statement from applicants, but I have my doubts whether a statement that is so obviously written by a confused applicant, with no outside help, would, in fact, be seriously considered.

Who would risk beginning their statement with the following introduction?

"I am really confused about what I need to write in this statement and how I can make myself seem interesting and committed to my chosen course. I think that I would enjoy studying XYZ but as I have never studied this subject before I honestly cannot be certain. I could pretend that I have read numerous books on the subject, like everybody else does, but this would not be true. I personally do not think that the cost of £9000 a year is worth it, but my parents insist that I need a university education. I am quite a good student and think that I would be able to get through this course and get a degree at the end.

Like the majority of students I will not get involved in university life and do not want to play sports or participate in plays and do not feel the need to lie about this. I realise that I am

---

[3] The Sutton Trust, *Research*, suttontrust.com, May 2014.

[4] Candy, S., *(Un)informed Choices? University admissions* practices and social mobility. London: Pearson, 2013.

not presenting myself as an especially desirable candidate, but I am essentially no different from the majority of applicants except that I am telling the truth."

Such a statement has the merit of being honest, but it would be described as naive and inappropriate and few university counsellors would allow it to be sent.

My personal feeling is that some admissions tutors would find the honesty of such a statement refreshing and would welcome the fact that, at least, it had been written by the applicant and not by a professional advisor. However, conventional wisdom dictates that the raw truth needs to be tempered and that qualities and attributes need to be presented in a modestly favourable light.

The second myth that I will address is the need to tell the truth. The example given above is an indication of how telling the truth is not necessarily advisable. That is not to say that you should lie, but you should not feel obliged to include 'incriminating truths'. In other words, the real reasons for wanting to go to university do not necessarily have to be stated.

> You are expected to **be positive about your desire to study** a particular course and to **express some knowledge** about the course and its content.

I do, however, believe that many admissions officers will appreciate honesty.

- e.g. to say that you want to study Business because you will be taking over the family business is not inappropriate and, at least, shows some long term aspiration consistent with the course. In contrast, to say that you want to study Law because lawyers can earn a large salary is probably not the best way to express interest in your course choice.

What to include and what to avoid

Having discussed some general points about the statement, it is now necessary to explore some of the important 'dos and don'ts'.

> **Clichés should be avoided** because they induce nausea and rolling of the eyes in most admissions officers.

The very worst of these is the phrase 'ever since I was a child' which claims an interest since childhood. No one will seriously believe that you wanted to be doctor since you saw a road accident at the age of three or that Philosophy has interested you since junior school. Even if this childhood interest happens to be true, it is best to present it in a more believable and acceptable way. It is much better to present your interest in a subject, either by linking it to the academic subjects that you are currently studying, or by linking it to an important current event or development.

Prospective Law students should not link their interest to a popular TV series or film, even if it happens to be true. It is much better to link the interest with some current event or legal issue that is controversial; such as the rights of minorities, or the importance of the rule of law. This type of link also has the advantage of showing your knowledge and interest in current issues.

For vocational courses, interest can also be shown by reference to appropriate work experience, even if this is part-time. A prospective medical student will be much more convincing of her commitment by helping out in an old people's home at weekends or being a volunteer for the Red Cross or Red Crescent. A year spent in Africa with 'Doctors without Borders' is best of all but it is not expected of the average applicant.

For those who are truly inspired by a particular course, it is essential to convey this interest in a believable way. The best way to do this is to discuss a current issue or development which will show that you take a knowledgeable interest in the subject and that you are familiar with such topics. Avoid making grandiose claims about books that you have read and their impact on you. Concentrate, instead, on new developments and the impact that you anticipate from these.

If your interest is Economics, it is better to present your view on a current issue, such as unemployment in Europe or income inequality, than to claim that you have been inspired after reading the works of Keynes.

Similarly, a History applicant should try to present an interest in a new development or interpretation that is controversial.

This applies to all subjects and it is only possible to claim genuine interest if some knowledge of recent developments is shown.

> You cannot be convincingly interested in a subject if you do not know what current issues are being discussed.

If you do not know what these are, you should find out by reading journals or newspaper articles. It is always better to display this knowledge meaningfully than to claim having read a book.

To say 'I am interested in politics and economics and read the Economist every week' might be true but it tells the admissions tutor nothing of value and cannot be verified. It is much better to make a reference to a specific issue that you have read about and indicate an interest in exploring this topic in greater depth at university.

If you are an EU or overseas applicant, you could refer to some event in your country that links up with the subject that you want to study. Similarly, if you have lived in different countries, you should show how this has given you a better understanding of cultural differences and an insight into alternative beliefs and attitudes. Universities welcome diversity and will want their courses to have a good mix of different cultural backgrounds. Speaking several languages and having lived in many countries makes you potentially interesting and these points need to be stated to show that they have contributed to your open- minded outlook. The fact that all IB applicants have at least one language, in addition to English, is a definite advantage and needs to be pointed out.

You should not present lists of achievements or interests because it sounds like showing-off and provides little useful information. The fact that you have volunteered to visit old people every Christmas since the age of 13 is very commendable, but it is much more useful to say how this has affected your personality and development. As a general rule, you should always mention an achievement or interest by saying how it affected you and specifically how it made you a better student or person. Many IB students participate in MUN and other international debating tournaments. To simply state this is not enough. You need to show how the experience had an impact on you. For example, having to argue a case that you do not agree with forces you to be objective. It may also enhance your diplomatic skills and your ability to speak in public. It is these skills that are important to mention rather than the event.

Similarly, with voluntary work it is important to say what you have gained from it rather than just mentioning it. All IB applicants have to perform some community service as part of their CAS programme and this is a potentially useful point to include in the personal statement. However, merely mentioning it is not the important point, but rather how this has affected you and made you a more accomplished individual. The ability to express your contribution modestly and with humility is very important, so you must never boast about such activities.

IB students have two further advantages, which should be mentioned in their personal statement. The first is the Extended Essay; this will hopefully be in the subject area of your chosen university course. Your aim will be to show how you enjoyed the challenge of researching your topic and how this prepares you for the skills needed at university. It is also an opportunity for you to emphasise your interest in a chosen subject area. If your Extended Essay is not in your chosen course area of interest, it can still be usefully referred to as an opportunity for studying a topic in depth, which constituted a challenge, by being in an area outside your 'comfort zone'. Even though the truth is that you chose to do your extended essay in History because it is much easier than finding a suitable topic in Physics, it is better to try and provide a more positive reason for this choice.

The second advantage for the IB applicant is the TOK course. This should prepare them for critical thinking and questioning of knowledge which are both skills that the universities value. The specific essay title that the candidate selects can be used as an example of a particular insight relevant to their chosen course of study.

How to structure the personal statement

The personal statement has a **maximum length of 4000 charact**ers, which roughly translates to **600 words**. You should not feel obliged to fill the whole space, but if applying to a highly competitive course you will probably need all of the space.

1. You should begin with a short introductory paragraph that attempts to capture the interest of the admissions tutor so that he wants to read on.

> Do not mention facts here that appear elsewhere in the application e.g. my name is Mary and I am applying for courses in Psychology... This information is already known.

Depending on how much of a risk taker you are, you can start with some humour. However, most counsellors will not let you take such a risk. A few years ago, an applicant for drama stated in her personal statement that she realised that as a dyslexic actor she would probably end up working in a bra. Whether the admissions tutors were amused or not is unknown, but she got offers from all her choices.

A safer option is to begin by describing the impact that a recent event has had on you and your desire to study a particular subject. Greek, Spanish or Italian IB students who are applying for Economics or Management type courses for example, can refer to the current debt crisis and the policy measures that are being enacted. This opening should be used to establish your credentials and justify your interest in your chosen subject.

2. You should then go on to link this interest to the academic subjects that you are studying and try to make some knowledgeable references to aspects of the degree course that you are especially interested in studying. Before making your choices, you should have gathered a lot of information about the courses that you are applying to and you should use some of this information to show your awareness of what the courses offer. A cleverly worded reference can also convey your first preference to a particular university.

Your aim is to show an enthusiastic interest in your chosen subject and this can be complemented by discussing any relevant work experience that you have undertaken. Again the emphasis here should be on how this experience has inspired you and deepened your desire to pursue a particular subject.

Many courses have a subject requirement such as Higher Level Mathematics for most Economics courses. When this is the case it is very important to express both your ability and interest in Mathematics and the type of topics that you are enthusiastic about. To do this you need to have carefully researched the course content of your choices.

Examples of actual personal statements of successful applicants

Example 1: Applicant for Education

Since embarking on the IB Diploma program, I have developed a much more inquisitive approach to learning and this has deepened my interest in education and the learning process. Why do I now like some subjects that I previously hated and why am I better at some subjects than others are questions that truly fascinate me. In addition, I am interested in the importance of the pre-school years to the education process and the significance of the home environment on academic development and achievement. All of these issues revolve around the formative years of childhood development and I am certain that this is the subject area that I want to study at University.

Note how the candidate explains exactly why they are interested in Education and how their experiences have contributed to this. Also note that their explanation is sincere and not exaggerated.

Children are the future and I want to be a positive influence on this future. I am confident that pursuing a degree in Education will enable me to achieve this goal and I believe that my background experience has prepared me for this academic pathway. At the age of fifteen I took the initiative to undertake voluntary work under the guidance of "Tandem", a non-profit organization motivated by the need for the improvement of quality of life of the children and adults with disabilities, the awareness of society concerning disability and social inclusion and the empowerment of vulnerable social groups. For two consecutive years I spent two hours a week working with under-privileged children and helping them in any way I could.

...And why we care is because:

The challenging situations that arose reinforced my desire to learn as much as possible, since I was able to ascertain the importance of education to a child's subsequent development. Additionally, in order to complement my practical expertise I did a three-week internship with a kindergarten, where I was responsible for assisting the permanent staff, in addition to supervising the children during the break and completing evaluation forms. This experience confirmed my belief that the early stages of children's lives play a catalytic role in their development.

Note that the professional and voluntary experience is presented in such a way as to reinforce the applicant's interest in and suitability for the course.

I believe that the IB program has been a good preparation for my undergraduate studies and it has helped me to overcome some of my academic weaknesses. Due to the numerous deadlines, the IB has enhanced my time-management and organizational skills.

Another vital skill that I have been taught through this Program is the Extended Essay. Having selected a particularly engaging topic, "To what extent has American cinematography reflected and shaped social attitudes towards mental illness?" I developed my critical thinking skills and was made fully aware of what a university education will entail.

Here the applicant has shown suitability for studying at university level

It is my firm belief that a good educator must be a versatile individual with knowledge of a wide range of subjects. I have endeavoured to broaden my horizons through several activities. For instance, classical ballet taught me discipline and dedication to something I love. Furthermore practicing the piano enabled me to realize how important a role music can play in education. I participated in the Student Unesco Symposium in 2012, which was entitled "The Transformation of the World". This experience gave me the opportunity to become aware of the global aspect of education and to exchange views pertaining to the topic with my peers.

I am very familiar with the organization and structure of British Universities having attended several summer courses at British Universities and I am confident that, given the opportunity, I will be able to make the most of my studies in the UK and make a valuable contribution to the shaping of children's future through education. There is no doubt in my mind that Britain is the place, where a sound educational basis can be formed on which to build for the future.

Example 2: Applicant for Engineering and Management

Whether on the Rugby field or in the classroom, I relish a challenge and will pursue success with great determination. Rugby and physics are two of my passions and for me are closely linked. As a relatively small person, the laws of physics allow me to successfully tackle much larger and heavier opponents by tackling low and using their weight to my advantage. Similarly the maximum effectiveness of the scrum can only be achieved by pushing together at the correct angles. It is this type of practical application that makes physics a fascinating subject and by extension the study of engineering.

Note that humour is good but make sure the joke is actually funny! And not just in your country and family! To be able to laugh a little at yourself shows confidence, but make sure your comments are authentic.

I have had the opportunity of working on some engineering projects and spent two weeks in the desert in Oman at the Schlumberger headquarters. What impressed me most was the leadership qualities necessary for coping with the hostile environment, together with the technical knowledge required for the project. Such projects can only be successfully completed if the project manager has both these skills.

That is when I realised that good management skills are as important as technical knowledge, in the same way that a good captain who inspires teamwork is a major asset for a rugby team.

Note how the applicant shows exactly what was learnt from this experience.

I asked the site manager which part of his academic training was the most useful for his current position and he said that the management skills were the most important and in particular the human resources skills. Characteristically he said that you can use mathematics to calculate stress and fatigue for cement foundations or steel columns, but you need a different ability to calculate stress and fatigue of workers.

Note how the applicant has researched into the field he wishes to study.

These experiences have sharpened my determination to study Engineering with Management and I am certain that both these subjects will fully satisfy my academic ambitions.

My higher level subjects in the IB are very appropriate for this type of course and I am looking forward to the prospect of applying mathematics to economics at university. The IB approach to learning, with its emphasis on free thinking and searching for knowledge and linking subjects together through the theory of knowledge has drawn me towards multidisciplinary studies.

I find the higher level maths and physics courses to be both stimulating and challenging while economics provides an insight into the current crisis affecting the global economy.

I believe that I have the academic training and discipline that will ensure the successful completion of my undergraduate studies and having carefully researched the courses that I am applying to, I am certain that they are exactly what I am looking for.

Having played Rugby for Harlequins at Academy level for the past two years, I can safely claim that I will make a positive contribution to the University team even if my academic contribution goes unnoticed.

Example 3: Applicant for Politics

Although I was too young to remember or understand the significance of the break-up of the Soviet Union and the demolition of the Berlin Wall I was harshly introduced to the world of politics when... [Information removed to respect the student's privacy].

Naturally, this family episode stimulated my interest in the events of that period and when I got older I was fascinated to read about it and previous periods of Russian and world history. At the age of 13 I attended an international boarding school and was able to have access to English language books on history and politics. This was a major eye opener for me as I realised that the same events can be shown in a very different light depending on who is writing about them. The more I read, the more I began to understand the importance of international relations in the global economy and the more I observed my President's political aspirations the more I understood that politics is the study of power.

As my studies progressed in the IB diploma program, I was able to add Economics to History as Higher Level subjects, and this complemented my understanding of important historical events such as the Great Depression and the forced industrialisation of the Soviet Union. What has greatly impressed me is that my knowledge of history, economics and politics allows me to understand issues which were previously unfamiliar to me, such as the Arab-Israeli conflict and the involvement of the Soviet Union and now The USA and Britain in Afghanistan.

I eventually want to follow a career in politics and hope that as a post Soviet person I will be able to offer a fresh approach and help to replace corruption and nepotism with a system based on merit and the rule of law. This might sound naïve and pretentious but as a young person I have to try to make a difference and stand up for my beliefs like some brave people in Russia are doing.

In order to pursue my passion for international relations, I participated in Model United Nations, which gave me a chance to take part in 3 conferences, in different parts of the world. It was captivating to be involved with international students my age, engaging into academic debates about global issues, and coming up with solutions to on-going conflicts, and crisis. The MUN conference hosted by Harvard in Beijing particularly had a significant impact on my view of the world politics. As it was the first occasion on which I have encountered political views of Asian students and heard their priorities in Global concerns. I found out about their main worries for the future of our world, and their attitudes towards globalization, poverty, and international diplomacy. After this experience I was able to make more connections between attitudes from all regions, and add key pieces to the puzzle of global politics.

In addition, I have gained some work experience, in the Russian Senate, in the department of foreign affairs, where I took part in organising a Russian-Chinese Business and Economics summit that took place in Omsk, Siberia in October 2013. It was a very educational experience as I witnessed the negotiations process, and learnt about organization of official events according to the protocol.

I have also done an internship, during the Festival of Russian Culture in France, which was hosted by the Russian Ministry of Culture. During this experience I learnt about different cultures and attitudes and I also improved my translating skills, in French, English and Russian. As a result of these two experiences, I now have a much better insight into the distinctive cultural characteristics of different countries.

This Personal Statement is very interesting because it uses a strong personal experience to show the applicant's deep interest in the subject. Personal stories that are truly powerful and genuine can make your Personal Statement very strong so if you have one use it.

However, the average student will not have a fascinating story. If you don't, just explain truthfully why you are interested in the course rather than trying to exaggerate personal experiences.

Now look at the following examples and see if you can pick out their strengths. I would advise you to pick the most suitable one and use it as a template if you are struggling to write your first draft.

Example 4: Applicant for Business and Economics

Having witnessed the collapse of the Greek economy and the closure of thousands of companies and businesses in recent years, it might seem surprising that I want to study Business/Management with Economics. I have two main reasons for this choice.

The first is that, apart from being my favourite subject, Economics at Higher Level has provided me with the opportunity of conducting research for an Extended Essay in which I examined the effects on local businesses of the recession and the recent VAT reduction on catering and food. As a result of this research I was able to see how economic theory is applied in practice, but more importantly I saw how different firms were affected and why some closed while others survived. It was also evident that some businesses actually did well in the recession and this emphasised that there are always some business opportunities, regardless of the economic climate.

The second is that my father has been a successful businessman and has managed to survive the recession by cutting costs and increasing productivity in the restaurant and bar that he operates. Over the past three years I have spent most of my summer vacations working in the restaurant in every capacity and have a fairly good idea of what makes a successful business. The decision to cut prices proved to be crucial as well as the restructuring of the style and menu from up market to cheaper All-Day convenience food. As I was directly involved in these decisions and observed how they played out, I am confident that I have a fair understanding of business practices. What I want to do now is to explore the applied theory and strategic analysis that is offered in my course choices. The option of Human Resource Management is of particular interest to me because I have become very aware of how important it is to have a happy and dedicated work force in the service sector.

Although I ultimately want to start my own business, I plan to get a good background in Finance and Investment and this has also influenced my choice of courses. I have always been good at maths and look forward to learning how to apply mathematical methods to economic principles and quantitative analysis. My other main academic interest is History and I am very aware of the parallels between past and current events having recently read about the Depression of the 1930's.

Apart from my academic interests I am an active member of various school teams and have won trophies as a member of the football team for winning the Private Schools

League and for coming third in the Pan Hellenic League. I participate actively in the CAS program of the IB and have found the volunteer work to be especially rewarding. I have good organisational skills and I am an elected member of the school council where I help to organise social functions and fund raising activities.

I have visited the UK many times and have had the opportunity of visiting all my University choices. I have friends who are currently studying in Britain and I have a very good idea of what student life in Britain is like. I am greatly looking forward to the opportunity of furthering my education with a sound undergraduate degree and sincerely believe that I will benefit from this experience.

Example 5: Applicant for Management/Economics

A Greek tragedy followed by a comedy of errors is unfortunately an accurate description of my country's economic policies and performance since 2008. Even my limited knowledge of economics is enough to understand that excessive increases in taxes are counterproductive to debt reduction since it only deepens the recession. Why is there such a high degree of mismanagement of the economy by first the government and subsequently the E.U. and the I.M.F.? The people responsible for the austerity measures are all highly trained economists but these same measures are widely criticized by other eminent economists.

These are the issues that I hope to be able to understand and discuss intelligently by following courses in economics, management and operational research at university. My favourite subjects in the IB are economics and mathematics and I look forward to combining these with advanced management strategies at university. For this reason, I have chosen courses which have options in management organization and systems analysis together with finance and accounting as well as structured courses in IT systems and applications which are increasingly important to modern business.

The IB has introduced me to a questioning approach to learning and I have adapted very well to this. I am interested to find out why theories that do not seem to work in practice are still part of mainstream economics. For example, the macroeconomic model, which assumes a vertical long-run aggregate supply at full employment, does not seem to have much relevance to the current economic situation in Greece. Over the past few years wages have fallen by around 30% but rather than falling, unemployment has more than doubled to 27%. I believe that the lack of productivity and competitiveness of the Greek economy is largely the result of bad management in both government and industry. Greek firms are very far behind in technological applications and innovation and have failed to invest sufficiently in research and development.

My ambition is to become part of a new generation of Greek entrepreneurs who will steer the economy towards sustainable growth through sound ethical business practices and management strategies. What I hope to learn from my undergraduate studies are the principles of good management and the integration of IT to strategic decision-making. I am fascinated by the potential application of 3D printing and the scope that it provides for manufacturing that does not require cheap labour.

I have chosen to do my extended essay in economics and my research topic is related to the impact of the recession in the Greek economy on the fast food delivery market in a northern suburb of Athens. I have enjoyed conducting the research for this topic since it provided a good opportunity of applying economic theory in practice. I believe that the research techniques that I have learned from this will greatly improve my performance at university and will prepare me suitably for the typical course work assignments and dissertation options available in my chosen courses.

With respect to my non-academic achievements, from the age of 16 I was selected for the Greek national under-21 5-a-side football team. This was a great honour but it meant that I had training for my school team, training for the national team together with 4 games each week. In addition to football I also participate fully in the CAS programme of the IB and have offered my services as a volunteer fire fighter. Although these activities have placed intense pressure on my time, I was determined not to let it detract from my IB studies. I am proud of the fact that I have never missed a deadline, nor failed to hand in an assignment on time and have managed to maintain a good overall standard in all my IB subjects. All these commitments have forced me to be extremely organized and disciplined and these are attributes that I believe will serve me well in my undergraduate studies.

Example 6: Applicant for Civil Engineering

My uncle is a civil engineer and has a construction company, and for the past few years I have worked for him during the holidays. Last summer for the first time I worked full time for a paid wage and was engaged in a road building project in the north of Greece. I was able to experience different aspects of the construction industry and realized the importance of organization and team work. Though the work is strenuous and sometimes dangerous, I found it to be very exciting and the experience convinced me of my desire to become a civil engineer and to study this subject at University.

My school grades are good enough to get into a good university in Greece, but I have decided to apply to British universities because the courses are more rigorous and the facilities are superior to those in Greece. Having spoken to engineers in Greece their advice was to study in Britain as the best preparation for working in a construction company. While at University I plan to continue working during the holidays to gain more experience.

At school I have always enjoyed mathematics and science and these are my best subjects.

In particular I have got good grades in Physics and I enjoy the practical relevance of this subject to engineering problems.

I consider foreign languages to be important and I have kept up with my German and English studies by attending courses out of school. I have also followed courses in Economics and hope to be able to combine some management courses in the future as this is an important part of a construction business.

During my school years, I have taken part in several activities. I enjoy sports like football, water polo and swimming. I have also taken part in numerous swimming tournaments all over Greece. Taking part in water polo tournaments helped me realize how important team work is and also the importance of good training and preparation.

I am looking forward to studying in Britain as I will have the opportunity to meet other people from all over the world and I am interested finding out about their culture. Having visited England and having cousins who are currently studying there, I am certain that I will settle in quickly and will make the most of my opportunities.

Example 7: Applicant for Law

Apparently I have always been inquisitive and my frequent recourse to "why" has brought some of my teachers to the verge of exasperation. Fortunately however, this inquisitiveness bolstered my strong interest in philosophy, politics, and economics and at last through the IB program I have been encouraged to question many things.

My institutional education in philosophy comprises knowledge from debate camp where as a Lincoln-Douglas (LD) debater I was required to research a utilitarian theory of democracy. This both inspired my interest in philosophy and politics as well as a love of detailed research from volumes of Bentham and Rawls and laid the foundation for a successful debate career.

When not debating or reading about a peripheral topic, I may be found clearing my mind by galloping the cross country course or tutoring middle-schoolers in mathematics. The tutorial system resonates with me, for since I've needed to work a lot on my own, I am good at self-direction and enjoy helping others learn to be as well..

Debating has exposed me to all three subject areas that interest me and the techniques I have learned have been valuable assets in performing well in IB History and Economics. After spending a few weeks immersed in the problem of dependency before a debate about the justness of American pre-emptive strikes, I found myself addressing the issue on a mock IBHL History exam and in one of my IBSL Economics commentaries. I like to think that I have a facility for understanding the questions posed to me by debate. Indeed, I am an avid follower of international affairs, devouring *The Economist* weekly and relishing the chances that I have to travel.

My summers are spent at academic summer programs or in another country – sometimes both – and I've discovered that experiential learning is my favorite kind. Last year, searching high and low for a unique article on trade agreements for my final

Economics commentary, I found Johann Hari's biting analysis of the World Trade Organization's (WTO) newest policy of eliminating special trade deals. I have always associated the WTO with seeking to decrease barriers to trade, but its actions as described in the article are antithetical to this purpose. Allowing less developed countries to continue taxing imports and subsidizing domestic production actually assists them in trading more freely. Developing countries exist in the third world because they are not yet in a position to trade freely.

I particularly enjoyed the emphasis in IB Economics on evaluation and the opportunity of questioning the merits of government policies such as cotton subsidies or supply side deregulation measures. The current world financial crisis has made such questioning eminently relevant and has exposed many accepted orthodoxies to detailed scrutiny

My personal experiences have also prompted me to question trade agreements such as CAFTA. Two summers ago I stayed with a family in Costa Rica while teaching English and helping to build a library. The elimination of tariffs on over ¾ of all American exports to the region would be disastrous to my host and the whole agricultural sector as they could never compete with multinational companies like Dole.

This first hand experience has increased my interest in finding appropriate solutions for development and I have explored the effectiveness of micro credit schemes which appear to be more effective than aid.

I have been fond of the free market since I absorbed The Wealth of Nations, but saw the exigency in American public policymakers' handling of CAFTA. Obviously only one interest had been considered, and I knew that I wanted to have a hand in resolving questions like these and that my hand would be an educated and cosmopolitan one. My career goal has since crystallized into being a lawyer for the World Bank or International Monetary Fund. Curiosity is necessary but not sufficient to accomplish anything, but a simultaneously pragmatic and philosophic treatment of the issue is.

Chapter 4: Oxford, Cambridge, Medicine and Interviews

Most admissions staff and tutors acknowledge that one of the best methods of selecting suitable applicants is with an interview. In practice, the logistics involved in conducting comprehensive interviews tend to prohibit their use and the majority of universities and courses do not normally invite applicants for interview. There are, however, some notable exceptions where the interview is deemed to be the decisive element in the selection process.

> Both **Oxford and Cambridge hold interviews for all of their courses** and state clearly that no applicant will receive an offer without having been interviewed.

Similarly, courses for Medicine, Dentistry and Veterinary Science invariably require that suitable applicants be interviewed before an offer is considered. There may be the odd exception, but for these courses you should expect to be interviewed. In all these cases, the interview is the final stage in the application process and you will only reach this stage if your application is considered to be good enough and if you appear to satisfy the other admissions criteria. Only a certain proportion of applicants are called for interview and you should not assume that being called for interview is automatic.

The Application Process

As already noted, the application deadline for these courses and universities is the **15th of October** and applications will be accepted from **September 1st** until this date. Both Oxford and Cambridge are collegiate universities, which means that you will not only apply to the university, but to a specific college of the university. You do not necessarily have to specify your choice of college when you apply and you can do this by making an open application, but you will be allocated to a specific college if accepted.

> Many applicants will have a preferred college, but you must **ensure that the college you select actually teaches the subject you wish to apply for**

You can find this by reading the university prospectus or consulting the web site. Those who do not have a preferred college may consult the listings of relative competitiveness of the various colleges for different subjects. Unofficially, some colleges are considered to be more prestigious for certain subjects than others. Nevertheless, you should not automatically avoid the most competitive college for a given course, because it might be the case that the majority of applicants do this with the result that the theoretically more competitive college has fewer applicants than previously.

Once your application has been received, it will be considered, initially, as with any other university, on the basis of actual and predicted grades, personal statement and reference. Applicants for these universities and courses will only be encouraged by their schools if they are strong enough, so it is to be expected that most applications are potentially good enough to secure an offer. The next step will normally be for some additional evidence of suitability to be exhibited. This could take the form of supplementary tests for Oxbridge such as the **Thinking Skills Assessment** (TSA) and in the case of medical subjects the **UK Clinical Aptitude Test** (UKCAT) or the **Biomedical Admissions Test** (BMAT). In addition, some Oxbridge colleges might ask for an example of written work to be sent to them.

Together with the information on your application form, these additional test results will be considered in order to decide whether you are a strong enough candidate to be called for interview. Note that not all Medical courses require additional tests so if you are not strong in this area you should only apply to courses that do not specify them. If your chosen course does have such a test requirement, you are strongly advised to consult the test web sites and do some of the practice tests that are available. The more practice you do, the better your final performance is likely to be.

If, after these initial stages, you are called for an interview, it means that you are deemed to be a strong applicant who is potentially worthy of a place. The interview will now be the final hurdle, after which the suitable applicants will be made an offer.

Oxbridge Interviews

As with many aspects of the application process, there is a colourful mythology that has grown up around the interview. If some of the stories were true it would put the trauma experienced during the interview on a par with the Spanish Inquisition.

It is generally acknowledged that stories such as the alleged incident of a student setting fire to the don's newspaper in response to the request: 'Do something to surprise me' are urban myths. Similarly, you will not have a rugby ball thrown at you to test your athletic ability. Entertaining as these stories are, they bear no resemblance to the typical Oxbridge interview.

The aim of the interview is to confirm the academic potential that you appear to possess. All of the applicants who are called for interview are potentially suitable candidates for an offer of a place and are quite similar with respect to their academic profile. The interview is your opportunity to show that you are suitable for the course and also provides you with the opportunity to judge whether the course is appropriate for you and whether you will feel comfortable spending the next three years in this type of environment.

All of the Oxbridge admissions tutors that I have spoken to are adamant that their aim is not to scare the applicant with impossibly hard questions or expose their lack of knowledge, but rather to give the interviewees the opportunity to display their ability to think and question.

> **They are not concerned to see if you know the correct answers**, but rather in your ability to examine and consider situations that you are not familiar with.

They want to test your academic potential by observing how you go about trying to work out an answer to a question, rather than whether you know the answer. To do this, they will ask you to consider theoretical situations or abstract problems in order to judge your deductive capabilities and your thought processes.

Sometimes, you will be given something to read before the interview and you will then be asked about your interpretation or understanding of some of the points that were detailed in the extract.

Applicants for **Literature** might be given a poem to read and then will be asked to discuss some aspects of it with the view to recognizing the applicant's ability to determine the meaning of the poem and the use of historical or other references.

Applicants for **Social Sciences** might be given an extract about the environment or a proposed government policy to read so that a discussion of the important issues can be pursued in the interview. Again, the aim will be to see if you can present your arguments and views in a coherent and convincing manner having considered the question from different angles. There is no right or wrong view, but there are various implications and parameters that could be identified and it is this skill that you are being tested on.

If you are a **Maths and Science** applicant, you might be given a problem to solve as a test of your ability, but again you will not be judged exclusively on whether or not you find the correct answer. The aim is to see how you go about trying to find the answer, in order to see how you apply your scientific or mathematical knowledge.

It should be clear by now that the aim of the interview is not to make you squirm because you do not know the answer to an impossibly difficult question. On the contrary, it can give you the opportunity of showing how you go about trying to find an answer, how you react to an unfamiliar situation and how you apply lateral thinking in order to try to deduce something meaningful. This is what they want to see in order to gauge your potential and ability to think beyond the facts.

A typical interview will be conducted by two academics familiar with the course you are applying for. There will, normally, be a second interview with two different academics and you might also be asked to stay around for an interview at another college. You will be given the option of staying at the college overnight, but you can travel to the college on the day of the interview. You should, of course, make sure that you arrive early enough to avoid unnecessary anxiety.

Staying at the college is recommended because it gives you a taste of college life and helps you to imbibe the atmosphere of the place. You might also meet other students with whom you can share your anxieties and impressions.

1. At the start of the interview you will probably be asked a neutral question to relax you and break the ice. Then, there will be a sequence of questions that will give you the opportunity of expressing yourself on familiar ground. This could involve some questions relating to points you have mentioned in your personal statement and, possibly, a brief discussion of your Extended Essay topic. It is essential that you are familiar with your personal statement and that you have actually read the books or articles that you claim to have impressed you.

2. Very quickly, the discussion will be directed to some issues relevant to your course with the aim of hearing your opinion and how you arrived at it. You might be asked about some current development in your subject and you should try to be up-to-date with such developments and with current affairs in general. You are expected to have some social and political awareness and to be able to discuss ethical issues with a degree of confidence and conviction. Some questions might aim to test your knowledge, but most will be aimed at testing your powers of analysis and clarity of thought and expression. Your opinion about an actual or hypothetical event might be sought and you should not rush to respond, but should take a minute or two to think about your answer. Do not be scared to ask for clarification if you have not fully understood the question.

3. At the end of the interview, you will probably be asked if you have any questions. You should take this opportunity to confirm your interest in the course and college by asking a pertinent question. This could relate to one of the optional courses that is offered, the structure of teaching or whether an interest of yours is catered for. Another alternative is to ask a question about your subject that has intrigued you and which has not been answered satisfactorily in your IB course. Showing interest and being positive is a good last impression to leave.

Some Tips

❖ Do not be late
❖ Dress in comfortable but casually smart clothes
❖ Do not answer monosyllabically but with sentences. If you do not know the answer to a question, say so but try to say something such as: 'I am afraid that I have no idea, but I would guess that …..'
❖ Try not to sound opinionated. Be objective and thoughtful

- ❖ Do not give the impression that you are well practiced with interviews and appear to be blasé
- ❖ Do arrange a practice interview with someone who knows the ropes, but don't overdo it. Just aim to be prepared to answer questions that you are not familiar with
- ❖ Try to steer a discussion towards your 'comfort zone' of knowledge and experience
- ❖ If you realize that you have said something stupid try to save the situation by admitting it and offering an alternative
- ❖ Be prepared for the predictable questions such as why you have chosen your particular subject

> Both Oxford and Cambridge have web sites that are packed with relevant information and **you are strongly advised to read these carefully.** You should also **look for articles about applying to Oxbridge** and this will help you build up a picture of what to expect.

> Recently, **both Universities have been willing to publish questions that have been asked at interviews** and there is considerable transparency about this, which will hopefully dispel the urban myths.

I have selected a sample of questions[5] that have been asked at Oxford college interviews with a brief description of what they intend to elicit.

Biological Sciences:

1. Why do many animals have stripes?

This is intended to generate discussion about potential advantages

2. If you could save either the rainforest or the coral reefs, which would you choose?

This aims to test the interviewee's ability to present a coherent argument and identify a variety of impacts.

---

[5] University of Oxford, *Undergraduate prospectus*, May 2014.

3. Is it easier for organisms to live on land or in the sea?

The interviewee must first consider the meaning of easier and then show an ability to assess relative problems.

4. Would it matter if tigers became extinct?

A 'yes' answer is expected but the 'why' is the most important part.

Biomedical Sciences:

Why do cat's eyes appear to glow in the dark?

The interviewee is expected to discuss possible advantages

Engineering:

How would you design a gravity dam for holding back water?

This requires some technical ability to apply maths and physics

English Literature:

Why might it be useful for an English student to read the Twilight series?

This is intended to test the interviewee's powers of literary analysis of non-exam texts.

Geography:

If I were to visit the area where you live, what would I be interested in?

This aims to test intellectual curiosity and ability to apply analytical concepts and awareness

History:

1. Imagine we had no records of the past at all, except everything to do with sport (or drama, or music) how much of the past could we find out about?

This aims to test the interviewee's use of imagination for linking familiar topic to historic research.

2. Which person (or sort of person) in the past would you like to interview and why?

This tests the interviewee's ability to match up the 'who' and 'why' appropriately.

Law:

1. What does it mean for someone to 'take' another's car?

This tests the interviewee's powers of reasoning and ability to consider hypothetical situations.

> **2. If the punishment for parking on double yellow lines was death and therefore nobody did it, would that be a just and effective law?**

This tests the interviewee's recognition of different issues and ability to distinguish between just and effective.

Materials Science:

> **How hot does the air in a hot air balloon have to be if I wanted to use it to lift an elephant?**

Here a correct answer is not expected. The aim is to test the interviewee's ability to identify important factors such as size, weight etc. and what mathematical techniques might be applied.

Medicine:

> **1. Why does your heart rate increase when you exercise?**

This question aims to elicit the simple answer regarding oxygen and then test more deeply with follow-up questions.

> **2. Why do we have red blood cells?**

This question is looking for a wider understanding beyond the basics.

The questions listed above provide the general idea of what the interviewers are looking for. There is rarely a correct or incorrect answer and most questions aim to test the ability of the candidate to apply knowledge, think laterally and identify interesting possibilities. The advice to all candidates is to relax and face the interview with an open mind. Do not over prepare but do have some practice as a test run.

Both Oxford and Cambridge provide videos of parts of an interview on their websites and a Google search will provide examples of mock interviews for certain subjects. These might be helpful, but do not over prepare for the interview. Have an idea of what to expect but remember it is important to have a fresh open mind that can engage with the unfamiliar and the unexpected.

Medicine and Related Subjects

IB applicants for medicine are sometimes at a slight disadvantage because their school only allows them to take two science subjects, which will inevitably be Biology and Chemistry.

Some medical schools prefer applicants to have Physics, as well. A-Level applicants will typically offer these three subjects at A-Level, together with A-Level Maths. You should however, be aware that you can get special permission to take three science subjects if you are applying for medicine. Alternatively, you could take a GCSE in Physics or sit for the A-Level or AS-Level. You might consider one of these alternatives if you want to strengthen your application, but it is by no means essential. Many IB applicants have been accepted for medicine with just Higher Level Biology and Chemistry and Standard Level Maths. Some medical schools even prefer candidates to have a wider breadth of subjects, including social science and humanities. Before applying, you should check the university prospectus and the entry requirements. If you are still in doubt, contact the department, either by email or phone, to ask what their policy is regarding subjects offered and if they have a preferred combination. You should also check whether they require additional tests like UKCAT. If so, make sure you do some practice questions.

The grades required for medicine are not excessively high and will normally be in the range of 35 to 39. What is crucial is a personal statement that clearly shows your desire to study medicine and your suitability for the course. Many applicants will have taken a gap year to gain suitable work experience. Although extremely advantageous, it is not essential to work with 'Doctors Without Borders' in Africa or something similar. Helping out in a local clinic or hospital or old people's home is also valuable and acceptable.

You should not just list this experience but you should discuss it with respect to how it impacted on you and your desire to study medicine as well as confirming your suitability for the course.

> If you do not take a gap year you will not necessarily be disadvantaged, but you **should still have some suitable work experience gained at weekends or during holidays.**

> Try to give a realistic reason for wanting to study medicine or dentistry and **DO NOT** use the phrase 'ever since I was a child....'

Having parents or family who are doctors is a good reason and it can link up convincingly with your awareness of what the training involves and the sacrifices that have to be made. If this is not the case, it would be sensible to refer to your work experience and the satisfaction you received. It would be inappropriate to say that the medical profession will offer you a high salary and a good job prospect, even though this might be your true motivation. A particular experience of a family illness or accident might be what stimulated your interest but if this is the case, you must be careful not to sound too melodramatic.

An alternative is to describe an interest in medical research and the prospect of adapting new technology and developments. You will need to be able to show knowledge of new breakthroughs and techniques and so reading contemporary journals is essential.

Your personal statement has to show your interest in the subject and your suitability and experience. Your academic interests are also important and you should state any particular field of interest, such as genetics or stem cell propagation, that you might have. In addition, a brief mention of your other interests is useful, such as music or dance or riding. You might even refer to their potential therapeutic attributes. The selectors will be looking for a well rounded individual who also has interests outside the field of medicine. Your extracurricular activities can also be used to show your leadership qualities and commitment. You need to show an awareness of the hard work involved in completing a medical degree and your capacity for this.

With a good personal statement, a good reference and convincing work experience, there is a good chance that you will be called for interview.

Interviews for Medicine

An interview for Medicine is likely to be rather more specific than those outlined in the previous section. Although some questions will be of a general nature, the majority will be more knowledge-based aiming to test your understanding of Biology and Chemistry, as well as your medical perception.

You will be asked about your personal statement and your work experience and you need to be convincing in your responses showing how you have benefitted from the experiences that you have described. You need to display compassion and empathy with patients, while at the same time showing strength and willpower to overcome emotion. Describing personal experiences from your work or volunteer service will enable you to convey these attributes.

Be prepared for questions such as why you have selected medicine instead of nursing. Your reply should not in any way belittle nursing as a profession and you should provide good reasons for wanting to become a doctor. An interest in medical research or surgery could be a possible valid reason. Bear in mind that many of the reasons you might give for wanting to become a doctor would apply equally well to nursing.

You should be prepared to answer questions relating to medical ethics and to express an opinion on issues such as cloning, euthanasia, and abortion. You might be presented with hypothetical situations to judge how you would act or react; for example, if the parents of a child refused to allow you to perform a life saving blood transfusion on religious grounds.

It would also be an advantage to have some knowledge of the British **National Health Service** (NHS) as it is currently undergoing important review and funding assessment. If you are a non UK applicant, some knowledge of your own country's health system would be advisable. You should also have some idea of how to assess a national health system and be able to identify strengths and weaknesses.

Unlike in other interviews, which mainly concentrate on establishing academic ability and powers of analysis, the interviewers for medicine will also be interested in your body language and temperament. A degree of timidity and anxiety will be expected, but to become a successful doctor you must be decisive and able to inspire confidence in patients. Your potential bedside manner will be under scrutiny, as well as your character and charisma. You must express yourself clearly and try to display a thoughtful and amiable disposition. Above all you must be sincere and eager to embark on this demanding profession. The way that you present your personal experiences is clearly going to be an important factor in demonstrating your suitability. Finding yourself in a difficult situation says nothing about you, what is important is how you deal with the situation and what you learn from it.

Some universities are increasingly favouring a technique known as **Multiple Mini Interviews** (MMI) where the candidate is taken round a circuit and presented with a variety of situations, some real and some with actors. The aim is to allow for a more objective assessment of your reactions and to limit the advantage that interview preparation may have for private school applicants. By presenting a variety of situations, it gives candidates a chance to compensate for a bad performance in one situation and provides the basis for an objective overall evaluation of their suitability. The questions that are presented do not have a right or wrong answer but, as with the Oxbridge formula, you are judged on how you react to the situations. The questions are likely to be of a general nature and do not necessarily involve medical knowledge, but rather will test your handling of the situation. According to Sara Doherty, of St. Georges University "It's a practical assessment...Candidates have to show us what they're capable of doing, rather than tell us."[6]

It remains to be seen, whether this style of interview will replace the traditional type or whether any new style will be developed. Whatever the interview form however, it is likely that the aim of the interview will be to test the traditional values of motivation, ethics, empathy and decisive communication skills.

Most universities provide detailed information in their prospectus and websites about the whole selection procedure and students are recommended to conduct an exhaustive research before finalizing their application.

Cardiff University presents the following information for potential applicants:[7]

---

[6] The Guardian, *Applying for medicine? Get ready for the new-style Interview*, theguardian.com, 7 October, 2013.

[7] Cardiff University, *School Selection Procedures-Medicine*, cardiff.ac.uk accessed 8 May 2014.

❖ In the 2012 intake round the University received more than 2,450 applications for 309 places; of these approximately 900 were invited for interview.

❖ Applicants who meet the minimum academic requirements are assessed on non-academic criteria according to the information contained in their personal statement and the referee's report. Applications are reviewed by trained selectors and the following are assessed and scored:

- Medical motivation and awareness of the career
- Caring ethos and a sense of social awareness
- Sense of responsibility
- Evidence of a balanced approach to life
- Evidence of self directed learning and extracurricular activities

❖ All applicants are expected to have an appreciation of the length of the training program and the career structure.

❖ No offers are made without interview. Interviews are offered to applicants who achieve the highest positions according to their academic and non-academic rankings (some degree of mutual compensation between these is allowed). The number of applicants to be interviewed in order to meet the student intake quota is determined at the start of the admissions cycle.

> **Interviews normally take place during a four-month period beginning in November**, and no significance should be attached to whether the interview date is early or late within this period.

❖ Those who are not invited for interview will be informed, through UCAS, that their application has been unsuccessful.

❖ Interviews normally last 20 minutes.

❖ The composition of the University's team of interviewers recognises the importance of balance in terms of gender and ethnicity as well as covering a range of professions associated with medicine. Each interview panel is drawn from this team and normally consists of 2 or 3 interviewers, at least one of whom is medically qualified, unless exceptional circumstances prevent the clinician attending. Panels may include a medical student from the senior years. Interviewers receive specific training and guidance on the form and conduct of the interview, including issues relating to equal opportunities and the benefits of diversity.

❖ The aim of the interview is to explore the non-academic criteria (see above) and to encourage applicants to talk naturally about themselves, their studies and their experiences, and to demonstrate that they have the interpersonal skills to be able to communicate effectively and whether they have a balanced approach to life. In this way they can show how they meet the academic and non-academic attributes required of a prospective doctor.

❖ Individual interviewers assess each applicant's performance and the interviewer panel agrees an overall recommendation.

❖ The final decision to offer a place is made by the Admissions Sub-Committee Selection Panel, chaired by the Sub-Dean for Admissions. It is determined by an applicant's overall ranking, based on a combination of the academic profile, personal statement and referee's report, and the interview performance.

Most medical schools will operate a similar selection process, though there might be variations in emphasis and selection criteria. Any such differences should be detailed in the prospectus and the website.

Chapter 5: Admissions Practices

In this section I will present the views of actual university staff who are involved in the applications and selection processes. A representative sample of Universities has been selected, mainly from the Russell Group, beginning with five that are part of the University of London and which constitute very popular choices for IB students. These five London universities are also those which feature in the case study referred to in chapter six.

The introduction of up to £9000 fees has influenced the selection and admissions practices of some universities and has intensified competition to attract the best applicants. Fortunately, IB applicants are generally regarded to be strong and some universities have revised their IB offers downwards, while others have introduced new scholarships and bursaries to attract applicants with high IB scores.

Of particular interest is the recent decision by **King's College London** to reduce all of its IB offers to 35 points overall, while placing greater emphasis on higher level subject scores. e.g. **7,6,6** for the most competitive courses and **6,6,5** for the less competitive courses. The equivalent A-Level grades are respectively A*, A, A and A, A, B.

According to Paul Teulon, Director of Admissions:

❖ 'King's is committed to a clear, fair and transparent admissions policy and want to ensure that candidates are considered appropriately and holistically. In the development of our new range of IB offers, we have to sought to reduce the potential unfairness which we feel may have inadvertently crept into IB offers in recent years. We are seeking to ensure that IB students, like students following other curricula, with the qualities to excel at King's are made appropriate offers.'[8]

The prospectus goes on to say:

❖ "King's has noted that despite the average IB student's grades remaining relatively constant throughout the past decade, for a variety of reasons the admissions requirements have increased. Our new range of admissions requirements seeks to redress this balance and ensure that IB students, like students following other curricula, with the qualities which will allow them to excel at King's are made appropriate offers."[9]

Oliver Selwood who is the Undergraduate Admissions Manager for Arts and Sciences at King's College further confirmed this IB friendly attitude. Despite being extremely busy, he agreed to be interviewed and happily answered my questions about King's selection process and the suitability of IB applicants.

The following is a summary of his views and responses:

---

[8] King's College News, *King's reviews its position on International Baccalaureate,* kcl.ac.uk, May 2014.
[9] ibid

❖ IB is the second most popular source of applicants, estimated to be about 20% of the total.

❖ Many courses are oversubscribed, so late entries are not usually accepted except in a few subjects.

❖ Admissions staff process applications and only marginal cases are referred to academic tutors.

❖ IB is considered to be rigorous and desirable for its wide range of subjects. The Extended Essay is important for some courses, as is the choice of subjects.

❖ Interviews are rare for Arts and Sciences courses, although courses in the Health Schools such as Medicine and Nursing interview as a matter of course.

❖ From the personal statement a sense of commitment is desired and references to the course are useful for showing preferences. Work placements are potentially useful and extracurricular activities are sometimes considered, but overall it is the desire to study a particular subject at King's that needs to be seen.

❖ The reference should confirm the academic ability and potential of the applicant and provide any important supplementary information which is relevant, especially to justify a high prediction for an applicant with a weak background. It is also important in flagging up any mitigating circumstances to b considered. Overall, it is felt that it is rare to read a bad reference, although this is one of the criteria used to make decisions on applications.

❖ The truthfulness of the statement and the reference, and the extent to which the statement is the work of the applicant is an important consideration and all necessary plagiarism checks are carried out. Admissions departments used software to do this, and it is also flagged up by UCAS.

❖ Since most courses are oversubscribed, very few clearing places are ever available and similarly very few adjustment places are accepted.

I questioned the new policy of giving all successful IB applicants a standard offer of 35 points and suggested that this policy runs the risk of encouraging applicants with a weaker academic profile, resulting in even more applicants for already oversubscribed courses. I gave the example of Business Management, which, in my opinion, would attract many more applications now that the offer has been reduced from 38 points and as a result the decisions about offers would be significantly delayed.

❖ His opinion was that the retention of high grades for the higher level subjects should minimise this risk.

The London School of Economics is a very popular choice for IB applicants, and for many the question of how to get an offer is one of life's great mysteries. The prospectus is very detailed with considerable information on the admissions criteria and the personal statement, but getting an offer remains a great challenge. Academic ability and potential is very important, but there is no shortage of IB applicants with 42+ predictions who are unsuccessful for courses that require 37 or 38 overall. Very often it will be the choice of subjects that is at fault. You should therefore, consult the website which provides a list of preferred subjects. For many courses, a 7 in HL Mathematics is required and it is advisable to include some indication of mathematical ability and application in addition to the prediction of a 7.

I was able to gain a more detailed insight into the whole process from an interview with Linda Hamer who is an Access & Admissions Specialist at LSE.

She explained that a system of filters is applied and that applications are examined as they arrive.

1. The first filter is performed by admissions staff who carefully consider the evidence of academic and subject specific ability. If this is seen to be inadequate, the application will be filtered out, unless the reference addresses the problem satisfactorily.

2. The second filter is holistic and looks at all the sections of the application. Experienced admissions selectors are involved in this filter and it is here that the personal statement will be scrutinised, in addition to the academic profile. The selectors are very skilled in spotting over-estimation of academic ability and can confidently distinguish between genuine personal statements and those with too much outside help. Above all, the statement has to convey a genuine academic interest in the subject and display suitability for studying at the LSE.
The Extended Essay is potentially useful. It is also advisable to provide evidence of knowledge and interest that goes beyond the syllabus in the key subjects. Appropriate knowledge of contemporary issues is desirable.

As will become evident from the case study in chapter six which follows the progress of an actual applicant, the LSE provides regular updates on the progress of an application until a final decision is made.

University College London is another popular destination for IB students, offering a wide spectrum of courses all of which are highly competitive. In addition to informal chats with admissions staff, I was able to have two interviews with academic tutors who take a very direct interest in the selection of candidates for their respective courses. The first interview was with Stephen Todd, who is Programme Director, BSc/MSci Management Science and Senior Teaching Fellow, Management Science and Innovation.

Management Science is a new degree course, with its first intake in 2014, and is looking for applicants with good mathematical skills, entrepreneurial drive and strong leadership qualities who can work well in teams. It is interdisciplinary, combining engineering principles with quantitative mathematics, economics and finance. The course attracted 735 applicants and about 180 of these will be made an offer anticipating an intake of around 100. IB applicants are considered to be highly suitable and the standard offer this year was **38** points with **6, 6, 6** at Higher Level, to include Mathematics. The Extended Essay is also recognised to be a useful preparation. As there is no shortage of highly qualified applicants, the personal statement is heavily relied on to identify suitable candidates. In addition, the applicants with the most potential will be sent a questionnaire to fill in, which has a variety of questions aiming to gauge the 'raw potential' that the selector is looking for.

Ideally, a mix of 50% UK/EU and 50% International is hoped for. The successful applicant will be able to work well in a team, sometimes leading and sometimes following. Qualities of entrepreneurship are important and the course encourages intensive analysis of innovation. The questionnaire attempts to identify these qualities.

The course is quickly developing links with foreign universities and with prospective employers reflecting its practical nature and variety. The course regards itself as a peer to Stanford and MIT. Furthermore, it aims to fill a perceived gap in the market for practical or vocational management learning.

The second interview was with Richard Pettinger who is Principal Teaching Fellow in Management Education | Course Director, BSc/MSci Information Management for Business | Management Science & Innovation. A summary of his views is presented here.

- ❖ **On the IB:** It is very varied - more so than A-levels, and so we are very happy to consider people from this background; it is an excellent grounding for University study (whether students come to do our programme or any other); we have a requirement of 36 as you know, which UCL equates to AAB at A-level;
- ❖ **Personal statements:** my advice always is - do it yourself! Don't go to a consultant or anything like that - statements that are prepared by others stand out a mile; structure and organise it so that the student says: why they want to go to a particular university (if it is one that has perceived high standing like ours then nod a bit in the direction of what is offered there); what they expect to get out of the course; what they are going to contribute to the course and the university; what else they would like to get from their university stay; and any particular achievements that they have had to date.
- ❖ **Interviews:** we no longer use them, though we will always meet with people either here or on their own territory (and our international office sends people all over the world to meet with prospective students).
- ❖ **Final decision:** a combination of all of the above; we make offers based on the whole application. Predicted final grades obviously help - but if someone was predicted low grades but the rest of their application 'stacked up' then we would make an offer. Similarly, if the predicted grades are very high but the rest of the application is poor then we would turn it down. So it all has to be right.
- ❖ **General appreciation of the IB:** we are all happy with it - it is universally recognised across UCL and we all look at applications with IB exactly as we look at A-levels.

Although not a member of the Russell Group, the **School of Oriental and African Studies (SOAS)** is a highly respected and competitive member of the University of London. As well as a wide range of language based courses, SOAS also offers courses in Economics, Law and International Politics. For Economics, the standard offer is 38 points overall with 7, 6, 6 at higher level, which is the same as LSE and UCL.

- ❖ I was able to interview Nick Butler, who is the Head of Admissions, and he began by stating that **SOAS** is very IB-friendly, valuing both the subject spread and the requirement of a second language.
- ❖ The selection process is centralised and as applications are received they are appraised according to a set of criteria, the most important being academic achievement and potential, as indicated by actual and predicted grades. If an applicant's academic profile is satisfactory, an offer will be made.
- ❖ In marginal cases the personal statement will also be reviewed and the application will be passed on to the relevant department for a final decision.
- ❖ Mr. Butler was the first admissions officer to openly admit that the personal statement was not of paramount importance but mainly used to choose among marginal cases. The assumption was that SOAS attracts applicants who have a particular interest in 'development' issues related to their chosen subjects and so a further interest or commitment as expressed in a personal statement is not necessary.
- ❖ What is essential is a strong academic background and evidence of the ability to do well on a rigorous and challenging undergraduate degree course. Some courses, such as Economics, Law, Politics and International Relations, are usually oversubscribed. However, admissions staff are very experienced and are able to identify those who are likely to do well and those who deserve an offer.

Unlike some other members of the University of London, **SOAS** is not reluctant to offer courses through clearing and is also happy to accept students through adjustment.

The fact that the standard offer for the most competitive courses is quite high, should discourage frivolous applications and attract only those who are aware of the rather special nature of the degrees. The philosophy at SOAS is : 'if you have the grades, we are happy to have you'.

Queen Mary College is a relatively new member of the Russell Group and has recently been creeping up the rankings in many subject areas such as Law and Medicine. Marlon Gomes, the Head of Admissions, is a very experienced and well informed selector who has an excellent knowledge of the IB and its equivalence to other qualifications.

- ❖ A steady increase in applications has meant some slightly higher offers. However, the aim is to keep the offers unchanged, as far as possible, in order to encourage applicants from state schools and from the local area.
- ❖ The typical offer for Law is still 36 points despite being very oversubscribed as a result of its top 5 ranking and this makes the selection process much more difficult.
- ❖ The selection process takes the form of recommendations by the admissions staff and course selectors make the final decisions.
- ❖ The admissions staff are generally trusted to identify those applicants with the correct academic profile and the course selectors will only need to decide on marginal cases.

❖ The policy is to view applications as they come in and Queen Mary is usually one of the first universities to reply to applicants. This is confirmed in the case study in chapter six where the first offer received was from Queen Mary.

❖ Furthermore, highly qualified applicants are offered attractive scholarships if they make Queen Mary their firm choice.

❖ The admissions philosophy is that the academic profile is the most important criterion and much weight is given to the predicted grades. In light of this, Mr. Gomes would prefer a post-results admissions process to the current pre-results offer system.

❖ In addition, he would support the introduction of extra tests by the Russell Group as a further source of information about academic ability and potential. Nevertheless, he is happy that the current system works well and that applicants to Queen Mary are dealt with fairly and efficiently.

❖ In view of the possible lack of transparency, the personal statement is seen as a potential landmine that often detracts from, rather than enhances, an application.

❖ Some courses conduct interviews for shortlisted applicants but most courses are not able to do this, except for special cases.

❖ Medicine is quite separate from the general applications process and is handled exclusively by the department. Interviews are always required before an offer is made.

All of the London Universities reviewed above are part of the UCAS process. However, there is another university in London that is independent of UCAS and is also discussed in the case study. It is the **New College of the Humanities (NCH).**

❖ Its founder and Master, Professor Anthony Grayling, is adamant that exam results are an insufficient indicator of academic suitability and that supplementary evidence is needed. In a written statement he presented the following views:

❖ "I am sceptical about the value of examinations, and even more sceptical about the validity of judging anyone's ability only on the basis of the numbers or letters on a piece of paper.

❖ Being an admissions tutor in higher education is a good basis for assessing how reliable exam results are as a measure of a person's true abilities.

❖ Because of the large numbers of students applying for university every year, most universities look at the paperwork only, and rely on grades as the final determiner.

❖ But if you interview candidates, read longer pieces of work they have produced during their studies, look at their curricula vitae and their references from their schools, a much fuller and much more accurate picture emerges.

❖ On that basis, a thoughtful institution can back its own judgment about the capacity of a candidate to mature and develop as a mind and a person, which is what the aim of higher education should be.

❖ The process just described is time-consuming and labour-intensive. That means it is expensive. For these reasons very few institutions do it.

❖ The result is a crude system of selection massively over-reliant on grades, made worse by the fact that the exam system, which awards those grades, is so deeply imperfect.

❖ In an ideal world there would be few examinations, and their use would be confined to getting students to sum up and bring together the fruits of their studies. At most the resultant grades would be indicative.

❖ Only the reading of longer pieces of work which have been more carefully prepared, and interviews, can really reveal genuine capacities and abilities; and these should be the basis of selecting students for higher study."

As a result of frequent discussions I have had with Jane Phelps, the Director of External Relations, and other admissions staff at the **New College of the Humanities**, I can confirm that they are extremely IB friendly and have a high regard for IB applicants who are considered to be especially well suited to the structure of **NCH** courses. This will also become evident from the case study in chapter six.

The standard offer is 36 points with **6, 6, 6** at Higher Level. For some courses specific subjects are preferred; for example, Economics requires Mathematics at Higher Level. However, applicants with Standard Level Mathematics will also be considered and if accepted, are invited to attend a Maths preparation course during the summer to ensure an appropriate level of competence in the mathematical skills required for the course.

❖ Part of the applications procedure involves the submission of a piece of work relevant to the subject. For this, the Extended Essay, or at least a draft of the Essay, is judged to be suitable because it shows the ability to develop analysis in an extended example of written work, as described by Professor Grayling.

❖ If the academic profile is good and the personal statement shows the necessary commitment and interest, the applicant will be invited to attend an interview. In certain circumstances, the interview might be conducted via Skype, but the preference is for the interview to take place at NCH so that the applicant is able to have a tour of the University and experience the atmosphere of the place.

This concludes the review of the six universities relevant to the case study. The rest of the chapter will examine admissions practices at some UK universities outside London.

Gareth Carey-Jones was able to give me a good indication of how **Exeter University** considers IB applicants. His views are summarized as follows:

❖ In common with most other UK universities we make offers to IB applicants in terms of total points as that is currently the way entry requirements for IB applicants are best understood. We have considered and will continue to consider moving to making offers differently, asking for grades in three Higher level subjects rather than an overall IB points score.

❖ The typical range of offers is 38 points for courses requiring A*A A to 34 points for courses requiring A A B.

❖ We work as a partnership. Criteria are agreed with academic tutors ahead of each application cycle. Those criteria are then used by admissions staff to make decisions.

- ❖ With respect to the personal statement, he referred me to the website which states: "The most important aspect of your application will be your achieved or predicted academic results, as this is the best predictor for success on one of our degree programmes.

- ❖ Personal statements will be considered, but mainly to identify any mitigating or extenuating circumstances that may have affected your achieved or predicted grades.

Where personal statements are considered more closely, we would want to see:

1. Your reasons for the choice of subjects taken at A level or equivalent and, where appropriate, the relevance of those subjects to your chosen degree course;
2. Why you have applied for a particular course and how this relates to your current and previous studies and experiences. If you have a career goal, it is helpful if you tell us how the course would enable you to fulfil that ambition;
3. Evidence of a willingness and desire to learn at a higher level: we are looking for students who have the potential and the drive to succeed;
4. Details of any work experience, paid or unpaid, and any other positions of responsibility that you've had. We're particularly interested in the skills gained from these experiences and how they relate to your own personal development and how they may help you in your studies and life at university;
5. Information regarding volunteering and other extracurricular activities and what you have gained in terms of experience and skills from these interests."

- ❖ Finally, adjustment is accepted depending on places and extra tests for non medical course are not used.

York is another popular Russell Group university and Lee Hennessy - Deputy Head of Recruitment& Admissions was able to provide the following answers to some questions:

Q1. How do you view IB applicants?

- ❖ Very positively.

Q2. Is the main selection process conducted by admissions staff or by academic tutors?

- ❖ Central admissions staff.

Q3. How important is the personal statement?

- ❖ The weighting given to the personal statement depends on the programme but every PS is read twice and forms part of our holistic assessment of the application. The difficulty is that we can never be sure whether it is wholly the candidate's work. We have to assume that it is and in some cases a strong personal statement will make all the difference between receiving or not receiving an offer.

Q4. Do you accept applicants through adjustment?

- ❖ Very few.

Q5. Would you like to see more external tests such as LNAT?

❖ The only external test we ask for is STEP for our mathematics programmes.

Birmingham University is looking to attract top students by converting conditional offers into unconditional for applicants with high grades or predicted grades who make the university their first choice.

Joanna Labudek, the Head of Admissions, confirmed that:

❖ IB applicants are treated in the same way as A-Level applicants and that the unconditional offer practice was extended to IB applicants as well. She went on to say: "We consider the qualification to be robust and believe that it prepares students for higher education."

❖ With respect to the main selection process, academic tutors set all entry criteria but for some programmes this is applied in practice by admissions staff on the applications we receive.

❖ The personal statement is important, for competitive programmes it is very important in determining whether an offer will be made, for less competitive programmes it can still make the difference between being accepted or declined if an applicant is borderline.

❖ Applicants through adjustment are accepted and external tests are not deemed necessary.

Although not a Russell Group University, **Bath** is a very popular, prestigious and competitive university. Lee Hennessy - Deputy Head of Recruitment& Admissions, was kind enough to answer the following questions:

Q1. How do you view IB applicants?

❖ Very positively

Q2. Is the main selection process conducted by admissions staff or by academic tutors?

❖ Central admissions staff

Q3. How important is the personal statement in the selection process?

❖ The weighting given to the personal statement depends on the programme but every PS is read twice and forms part of our holistic assessment of the application. The difficulty is that we can never be sure whether it is wholly the candidate's work. We have to assume that it is and in some cases a strong personal statement will make all the difference between receiving and not receiving an offer.

Q4. Do you accept applicants through adjustment?

❖ Very few

Q5. Would you like to see more external tests such as LNAT?

❖ The only external test we ask for is STEP for our mathematics programmes.

All of the above comments from admissions staff are quite typical and represent the general attitude to IB applicants which is invariably positive. It would be repetitive to include more universities with regard to general admissions practices for academic courses as the views of admissions officers are very similar with respect to IB applicants.

I will however, include a final report from one of the leading universities for Drama in the UK, the Central School of Speech and Drama (CSSD).

Ollie Mawdsley, the Admissions Officer, provided the following answers to my questions:

Q1. Is the IB held in high regard or are applications from IB candidates less competitive than A-Level students?

❖ IB candidates are held in no higher nor lower esteem than A-Level or BTEC candidates. We aim to give all candidates the same opportunities, as we are aware that success in our degrees is just as likely to be as a result of talent and hard work as it is of academic background.

Q2. Are applicants interviewed for all undergraduate courses?

❖ Yes, everyone is interviewed, as we believe this gives people the best possible opportunity to show us what they have to offer.

Q3. In your experience, who usually helps students prepare for their auditions?

❖ I assume you're talking about the BA (Hons) Acting auditions. Most of our applicants for this course are involved in a drama group of some sort, either as part of their school life or as an extracurricular activity, and in our experience, the people who run these groups are often more than happy to give up their time in order to help someone with the drive and talent to audition for drama school. For our other two BA courses, it's normally the drama or art teachers at school who help the applicants with their interview prep.

Q4. Do admissions officers or academic tutors conduct the main selection process?

❖ For all of our courses, the interviews and auditions are conducted by academic tutors at Central, both permanent and visiting staff members who have worked extensively on the courses here.

Q5. How important is the personal statement and how much does it influence the selection decision?

❖ The personal statement is important to us as a means of furthering discussion regarding the applicants' experience, interests and ideas. Due to our fairly intensive interview procedures, those with poor personal statements still have a chance to show us what matters to them, however it makes the process much easier all round if people are honest and passionate with their statements.

Chapter 6: Case Study

In this section, I will present the application process of a student of mine from the initial stages to the acceptance of offers. His name is Konstantinos Malamas and he follows the IB programme at a school in Greece. His personal statement is example 5 in Chapter 3. He kept a diary of the events and they are presented as a time-line as follows:

August:

As I am finishing off my Extended Essay I am beginning to think about my University choices. I am between Management and Economics, but some Economics courses require HL Maths. I am taking standard level Maths, but I hope to get a 7, which is acceptable for some Economics courses.

I am only interested in London Universities so my choice is limited. I have high predictions and expectations so I will apply to competitive Universities.

I have decided on the following choices:

LSE - Management

UCL - Information Management for Business

SOAS - Economics

King's College - Business Management

Queen Mary - Economics

Although these courses are related, I will have to be careful to appeal to all in my personal statement without sounding undecided or vague.

I will also have to try to convey my special preference for LSE and UCL.

I have decided to apply to NCH as well.

September:

Even though I have already visited some of these universities, I decided to arrange a more formal visit to discuss the courses with tutors from actual departments at SOAS, UCL and NCH.

My adviser arranges these visits for early September.

I was very impressed with UCL and was given a tour of the main building. The course sounds very interesting and dynamic.

After UCL, I visited SOAS and spoke to an Economics tutor and found out about the course and the various options. As expected, the course is weighted heavily in favour of development economics. I then had a tour of the buildings and was interested to see students queuing up for free food outside the main building.

The following day I visited NCH and was able to discuss the Economics degree with the Economics tutor and the Maths requirement with the Mathematics tutor. The emphasis is on small groups and weekly 1 to 1 tutorials. I was given a tour of the buildings and spoke with some students and staff who all seemed very enthusiastic.

October:

I began the process of completing my UCAS application and prepared a first draft of my personal statement. My adviser suggested that I include a bit more about my football achievements and to find some features of the two courses that interested me the most to mention. My second draft was much better and after correcting some clumsy expressions I pasted the completed statement on my form.

My application then went to the school counselor who collected views and predictions from my subject teachers and proceeded to write my reference.

November:

I submitted my UCAS application on 6th of November.

By 9th of November, I had received acknowledgement letters from all the universities of their receipt of my application.

On November 12th, I received a communication from the LSE that they are currently viewing my application and will contact me again in due course about its progress.

On November 21^{s,t} I received an offer from Queen Mary (35 points + 5 SL Maths)

After receiving a draft of my Extended Essay, NCH decided to interview me. This was arranged via Skype on 27th November. I was sent an extract to study an hour before the interview and was asked questions about this and the Extended Essay during the interview. I was then asked a variety of other questions to test my ability to interpret and evaluate.

December:

On the 11th of December, I received an offer from NCH (36 points).

On The 18th December, Queen Mary offered me a scholarship if I make them my firm choice and if I secure 38 points and 7 in Maths.

January:

On the 15th January, I received an offer from UCL. (36 points with 17 in HL and no subject less than 5)

On the 17th January, I received a communication from LSE, which said that my application was very strong and was being seriously considered and that I would be informed of a decision within 4 weeks.

February:

On the 4th of February, I received an offer from SOAS (38 points with 7, 6, 6, at HL)

On the 13th of February, I received an offer from LSE (37 points with HL 6,6,7 HL English and 7 SL Maths) Quite a stiff offer but welcome nonetheless.

16th February-still not heard anything from King's which surprises me given that they have lowered their IB offers to 35 points. Decide to withdraw application to King's since I have already got my two preferred offers.

March:

On the 12th of March, NCH changes my offer to unconditional and awards an exhibition so that my fees will be reduced to below 8000 pounds instead of 18000 pounds. This makes NCH less expensive than LSE and UCL.

On the 21st of March, I decide to finalise my UCAS choices: LSE firm UCL insurance.

April:

On the 9th of April I attend an open day at LSE. I find out more about the course and get a tour of the buildings. I also meet other successful applicants for my course and was interested to hear that several of them had been rejected for the IMB course at UCL.

All that is left now is to get the grades!!!!!!!!!!!!!!!, but the exhibition and unconditional offer from NCH is a big advantage and will relieve a lot of the exam pressure next month.

References

Candy, S., *(Un)informed Choices? University admissions* practices and social mobility. London: Pearson, 2013.

Cardiff University, *School Selection Procedures-Medicine*, cardiff.ac.uk accessed 8 May 2014.

King's College News, *King's reviews its position on International Baccalaureate,* kcl.ac.uk, May 2014.

Russell Group Website, russellgroup.ac.uk, 1 May 2014.

The Guardian, *Applying for medicine? Get ready for the new-style Interview*, theguardian.com, 7 October, 2013.

The Sutton Trust, *Research,* suttontrust.com, May 2014.

University of Oxford, *Undergraduate prospectus*, May 2014.

www.ingramcontent.com/pod-product-compliance
Lightning Source LLC
Chambersburg PA
CBHW080536290526
45790CB00006B/2432